More Christmas Piano Solos

For All Piano Methods

Table of Contents

ISBN 978-1-4234-8364-9

HAL•LEONARD®

7777 W. BLUEMOUND RD. P.O. BOX 13819 MILWAUKEE, WI 53213

Visit Hal Leonard Online at
www.halleonard.com

Santa Claus Is Comin' to Town

Words by Haven Gillespie
Music by J. Fred Coots
Arranged by Phillip Keveren

mak-ing a list and check-ing it twice, Gon - na find out who's

naugh - ty and nice, San - ta Claus is com - in' to

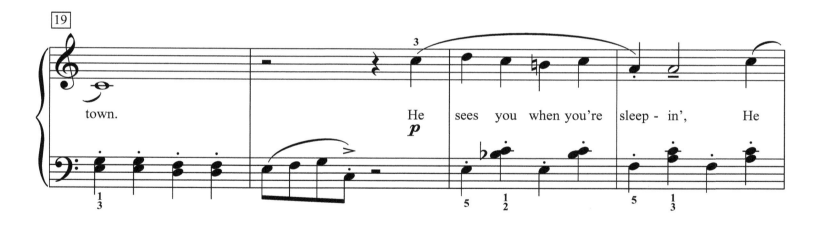

town. He sees you when you're sleep - in', He

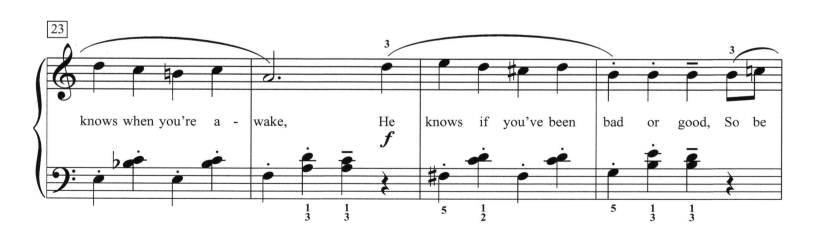

knows when you're a - wake, He knows if you've been bad or good, So be

3

good, for good-ness sake.

You bet-ter watch out, you bet-ter not cry, Bet-ter not pout, I'm tell-ing you why: San-ta Claus is com-in', San-ta Claus is com-in', San-ta Claus is com-in' to town!

Wonderful Christmastime

Words and Music by
Paul McCartney
Arranged by Mona Rejino

17 Sim - ply hav - ing a won - der - ful Christ - mas - time.

21 *mp* The choir of chil - dren sing their

25 song. (They prac - tised all year long.)

29 Ding dong, ding dong, ding dong, ding dong, ding

dong,   ding dong,   dong,   dong,   dong,   dong.   The par-ty's on, __

__ the spir-it's up, __   we're here to-night __

__   and that's e - nough. __   Sim - ply
                                                    sim - ply

hav - ing   a   won - der-ful Christ-mas - time.   We're
hav - ing   a   won - der-ful Christ-mas - time.   time.

What Child Is This?

Words by William C. Dix
16th Century English Melody
Arranged by Phillip Keveren

17

sleep _____ ing? Whom an - gels greet _____ with

21

an - thems sweet, _____ while shep - herds watch _____ are

25

keep - ing? This, this _____ is

mf

29

Christ the King, _____ Whom shep - herds guard _____ and

9

an - gels sing: Haste, haste ____ to bring Him laud, ____ The Babe, ____ the Son ____ of Mar - y!

rit. e dim.

O Come, O Come, Emmanuel

Traditional Latin Text
15th Century French Melody
Arranged by Fred Kern

us the path of know - ledge show and cause us in her

ways _____ to go. Re - joice! Re - joice! Em -

man - u - el shall come to thee, O Is - ra -

el.

13

Snowfall

Lyrics by Ruth Thornhill
Music by Claude Thornhill
Arranged by Phillip Keveren

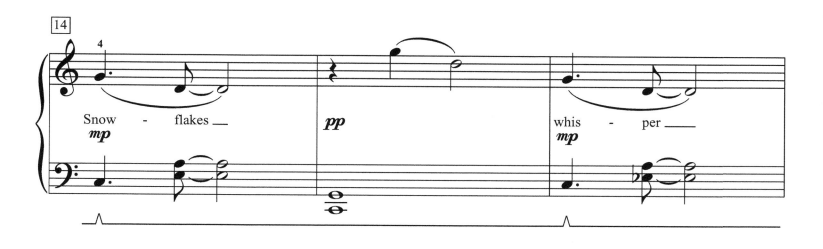

Snow - flakes _____ *pp* whis - per _____
mp   *mp*

pp 'neath my _____ *pp*
mp

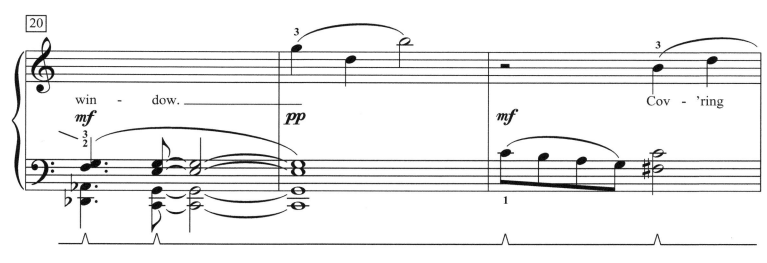

win - dow. _____ *pp* Cov - 'ring
mf   *mf*

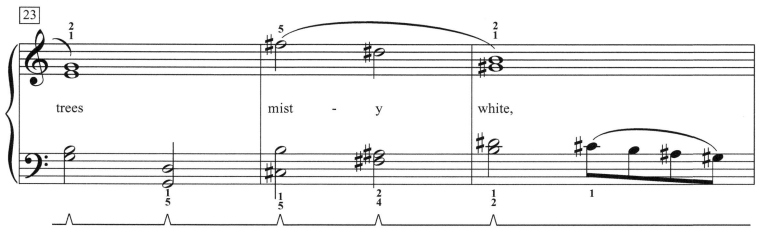

trees   mist - y   white,

vel - vet breeze 'round my door - step.

Gen - tly, _____ pp soft - ly, _____

pp si - lent _____ pp

snow - fall! _____ rit. pp

It Came Upon the Midnight Clear

Words by Edmund Hamilton Sears
Music by Richard Storrs Willis
Arranged by Fred Kern

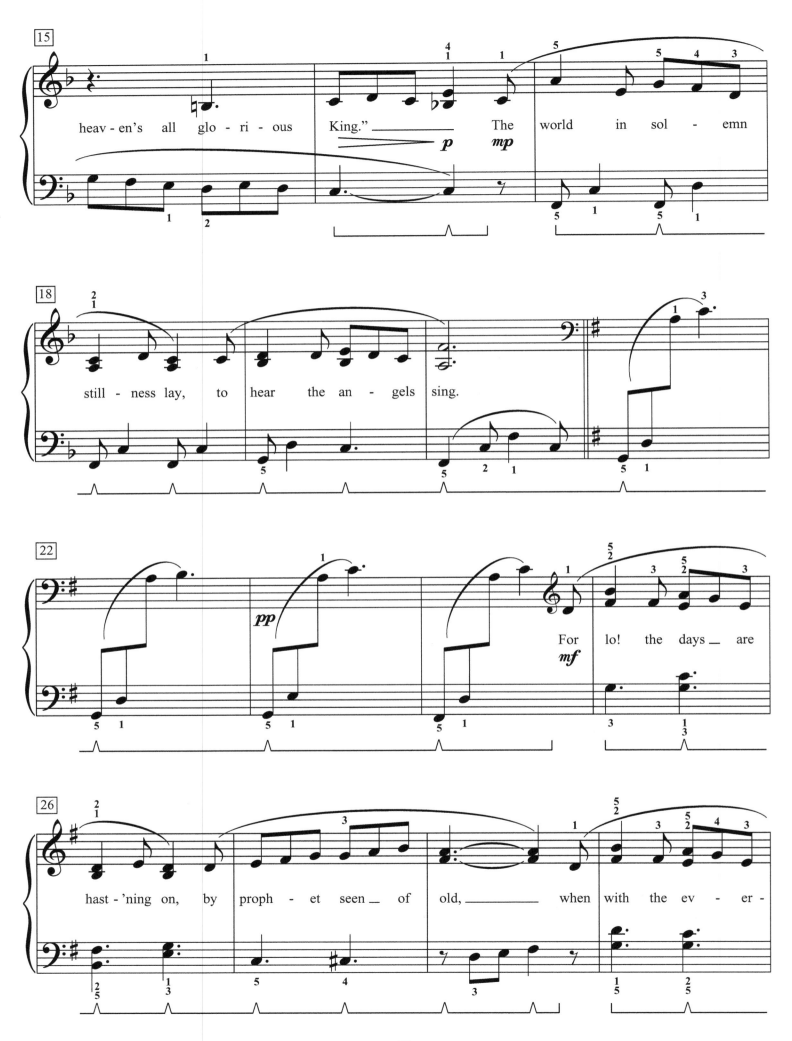

heav-en's all glo-ri-ous King." The world in sol-emn

still-ness lay, to hear the an-gels sing.

For lo! the days are

hast-'ning on, by proph-et seen of old, when with the ev-er-

cir - cling years shall come the time — fore - told — when peace shall o - ver

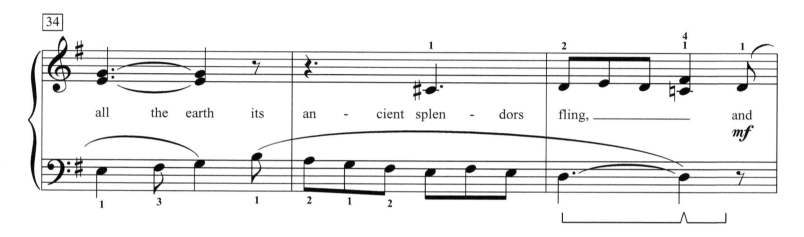

all the earth its an - cient splen - dors fling, — and

the whole world — send back the song which now the an - gels

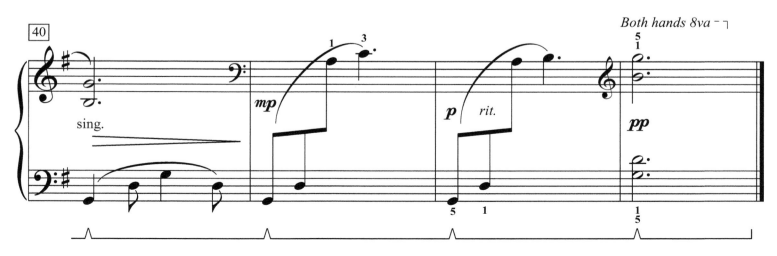

Both hands 8va

sing.

19

Grandma Got Run Over by a Reindeer

Words and Music by
Randy Brooks
Arranged by Jennifer Linn

as for me and Grand-pa, we be-lieve.

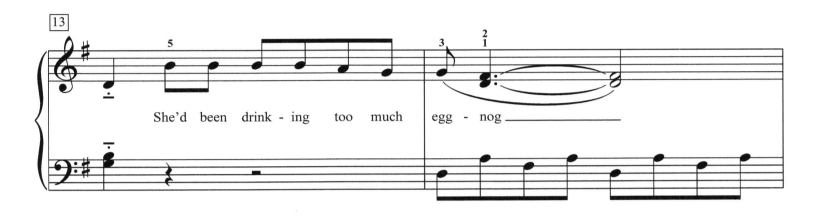

She'd been drink-ing too much egg - nog

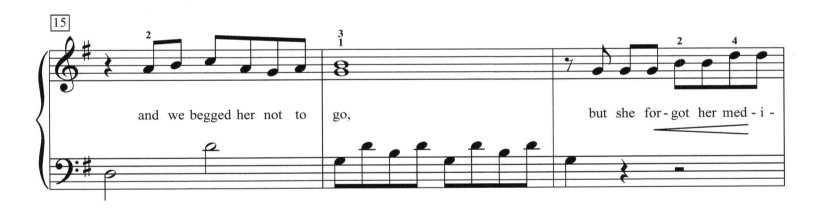

and we begged her not to go, but she for-got her med-i-

ca-tion, and she stag-gered out the door in-to the snow.

When we found her Christ - mas morn - ing

at the scene of the at - tack,

she had hoof - prints on her fore - head, and in -

crim - i - nat - ing Claus marks on her back.

Grand - ma got run o - ver by a

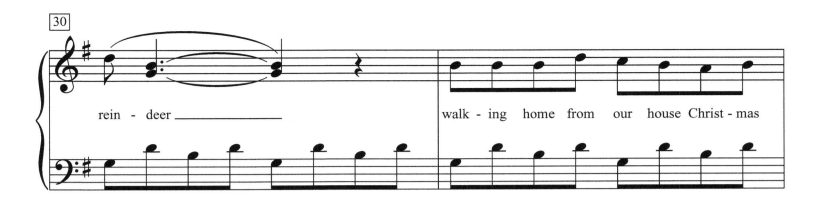

rein - deer _____ walk - ing home from our house Christ - mas

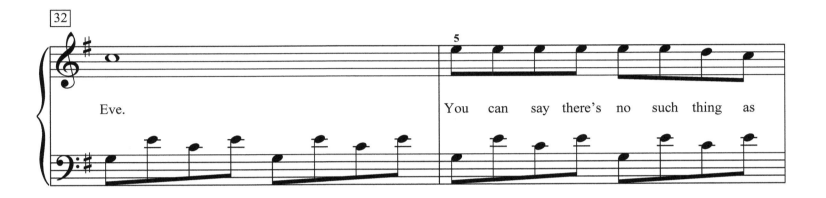

Eve. You can say there's no such thing as

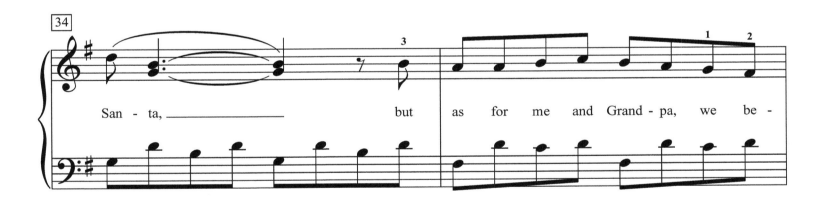

San - ta, _____ but as for me and Grand - pa, we be -

lieve. _____

f

Believe
from Warner Bros. Pictures' THE POLAR EXPRESS

Words and Music by Glen Ballard
and Alan Silvestri
Arranged by Fred Kern

dream - ers _____ not so long _____ a - go, _____
sail - ing _____ far a - cross the sea, _____

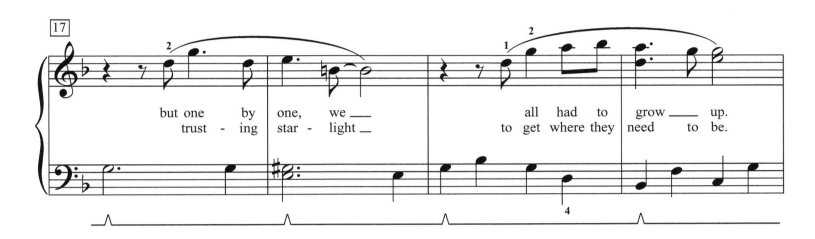

but one by one, we _____ all had to grow _____ up.
trust - ing star - light _____ to get where they need to be.

When it seems the mag - ic slipped a - way, we find it all a - gain on Christ - mas
When it seems that we have lost our way, we find our - selves a - gain on Christ - mas

mf

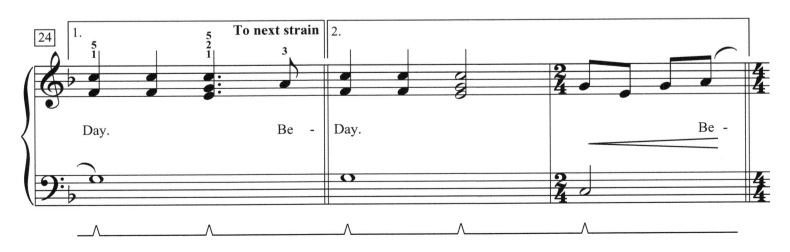

1.
To next strain 2.

Day. Be - Day. Be -

lieve in what your heart is say-ing, hear the mel - o - dy that's play-ing. There's no time to waste, there's so

much to cel - e - brate. Be - lieve in what you feel in - side and give your dreams the wings to

fly. You have ev - 'ry - thing you need, if you just be -

lieve. lieve. If you just be -

lieve,

if you just be - lieve,

if you just be - lieve.

Just be -

lieve,

just be - lieve.

Repeat and Fade

27

Bring a Torch, Jeanette, Isabella

17th Century French Provençal Carol
Arranged by Carol Klose

Both hands 8va the first time through.

Bring a torch, Jean-
Has - ten now, good

nette, Is - a - bel - la, Bring a torch, come swift - ly and
folk of the vil - lage, Has - ten now, the Christ Child to

run.
see. Christ is born; tell the folk of the vil - lage.
You will find Him a - sleep in a man - ger.

Je - sus is sleep - ing in His cra - dle. Ah,
Qui - et - ly come and whis - per soft - ly.

poco rit.

mp a tempo

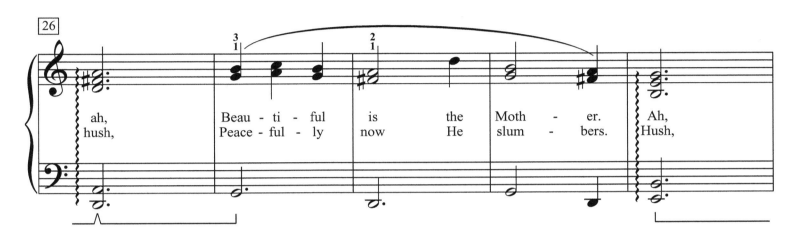

ah, Beau - ti - ful is the Moth - er. Ah,
hush, Peace - ful - ly now is He slum - bers. Hush,

1.

ah, Beau - ti - ful is her Son.
hush, Peace - ful - ly

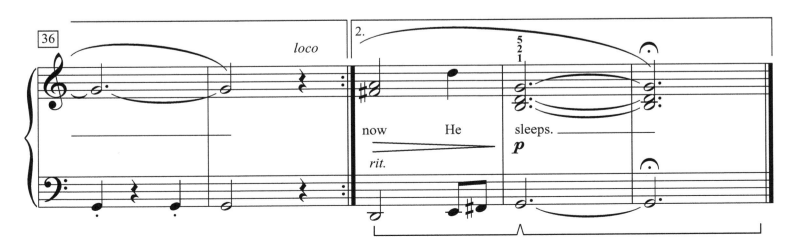

loco

2.

now He sleeps.

rit.

p

Lo, How a Rose E'er Blooming

15th Century German Carol
Translated by Theodore Baker
Music from *Alte Catholische Geistliche Kirchengesang*
Arranged by Mona Rejino

Lo, how a rose e'er bloom - ing, From
I - sai - ah 'twas fore - told it, The

ten - der stem hath sprung! Of Jes - se's
Rose I have in mind. With Mar - y

lin - eage com - ing, As men of old
we be - hold it, The Vir - gin Moth -

have sung.
-er kind. It came a flow'r-et bright,
To show God's love a-right,

A - mid the cold of win - ter, When
She bore to men a Sav - ior, When

half spent was the night.
half spent was the night.

rit.

Do You Hear What I Hear

Words and Music by Noel Regney
and Gloria Shayne
Arranged by Carol Klose

Child, the Child, sleep - ing in the night, He will

bring us good - ness and light, He will bring us

good - ness and light." *f*

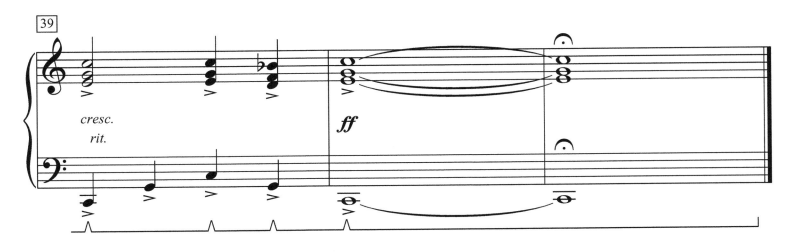

cresc.
rit. *ff*

O Holy Night

French Words by Placide Cappeau
English Words by John S. Dwight
Music by Adolphe Adam
Arranged by Fred Kern

Gently, moving (♩. = 56)

wea - ry world re - joic - es, for yon - der
grate - ful chor - us raise we, let all with -

breaks a new and glo - rious morn.
in us praise and His ho - ly name.

Fall _____ on your knees! _____
Christ _____ is the Lord! _____

f

___ O hear _____ the an - gel
___ O praise _____ His name for -

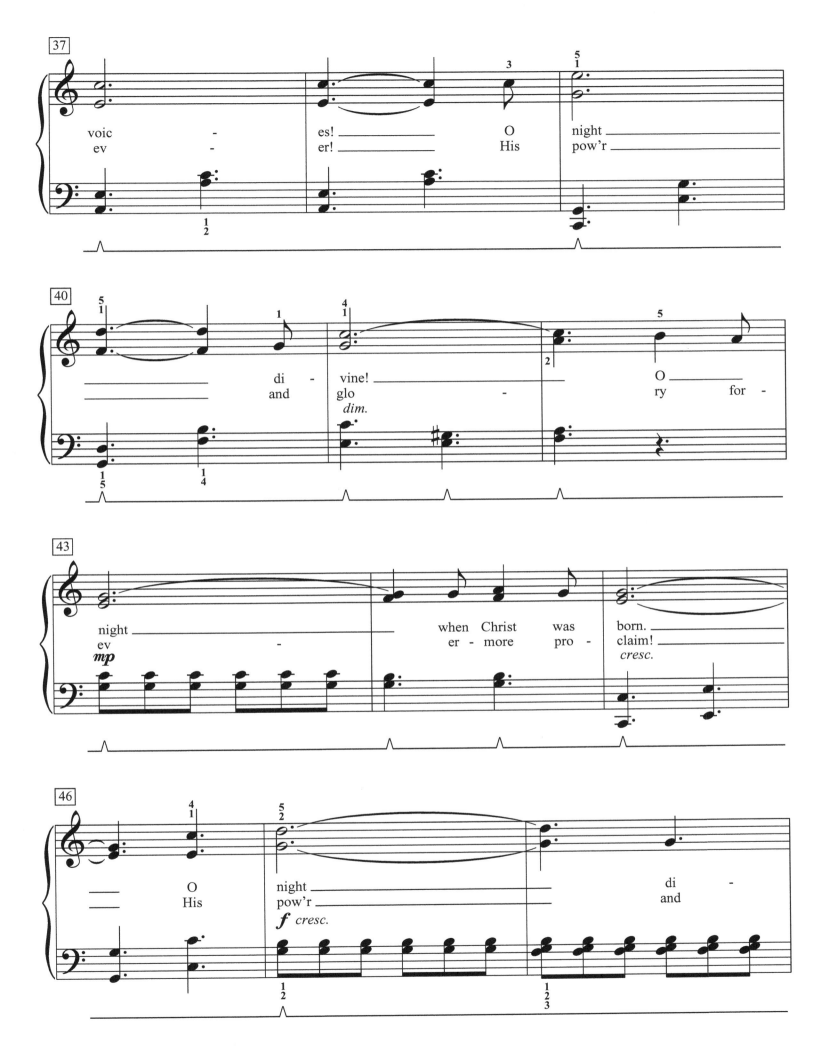